WORDS OF WISDOM

FRANKLIN DELANO ROOSEVELT

JOLLYJOY

100 Selected Quotes
by Franklin D. Roosevelt

Edition 2024

Published by

JOLLYJOY

G/F, 4771/23, Bharat Ram Road, Daryaganj, New Delhi-110002

E-mail: Contact@jollyjoybooks.com

ISBN: 9789363971042

Cover, Typesetting, and Book Design by JollyJoy
Printed & bound in India

ABOUT THE AUTHOR

Franklin D. Roosevelt (born January 30, 1882, Hyde Park, New York, U.S.—died April 12, 1945, Warm Springs, Georgia) was the 32nd president of the United States (1933–45). The only president elected to the office four times, Roosevelt led the United States through two of the greatest crises of the 20th century: the Great Depression and World War II. In so doing, he greatly expanded the powers of the federal government through a series of programs and reforms known as the New Deal.

100 SELECTED QUOTES

"The only thing we have to fear is fear itself."

"Remember, remember always,
that all of us, and you and I especially,
are descended from immigrants and revolutionists."

"I ask you to judge me by the enemies I have made."

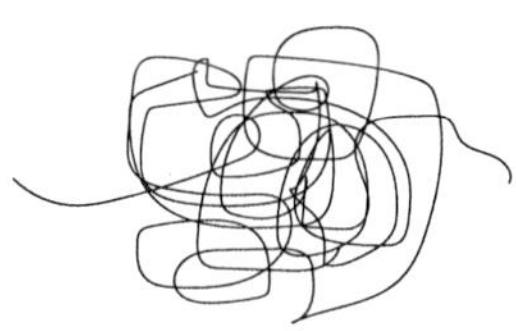

"When you come to the end of your rope,
tie a knot and hang on."

*"We cannot always build the future for our youth,
but we can build our youth for the future."*

"The test of our progress is not whether
we add more to the abundance of those who have much;
it is whether we provide enough for those who have too little."

"A nation that destroys its soils destroys itself. Forests are the lungs of our land, purifying the air and giving fresh strength to our people."

"Courage is not the absence of fear,
but rather the assessment that something else is
more important than fear."

"The liberty of a democracy is not safe if the people tolerated the growth of private power to a point where it becomes stronger than the democratic state itself. That in its essence is fascism: ownership of government by an individual, by a group, or any controlling private power."

"I'm not the smartest fellow in the world,
but I can sure pick smart colleagues."

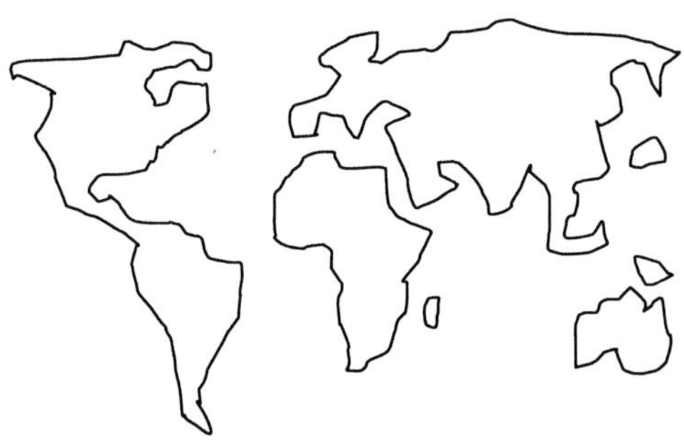

"To reach a port we must set sail
Sail, not tie at anchor Sail, not drift."

"Democracy cannot succeed unless those who express their choice are prepared to choose wisely. The real safeguard of democracy, therefore, is education."

"Books can not be killed by fire.
People die, but books never die.
No man and no force can abolish memory... In this war,
we know, books are weapons.
And it is a part of your dedication always to make
them weapons for man's freedom."

A
SMOOTH
SEA
NEVER
MADE
A
SKILLED
SAILOR

*"The only limit to our realization of
tomorrow will be our doubts of today.
Let us move forward with strong and active faith."*

"Happiness is not in the mere possession of money;
it lies in the joy of achievement, in the thrill of creative effort."

"Happiness lies in the joy of achievement and the thrill of creative effort."

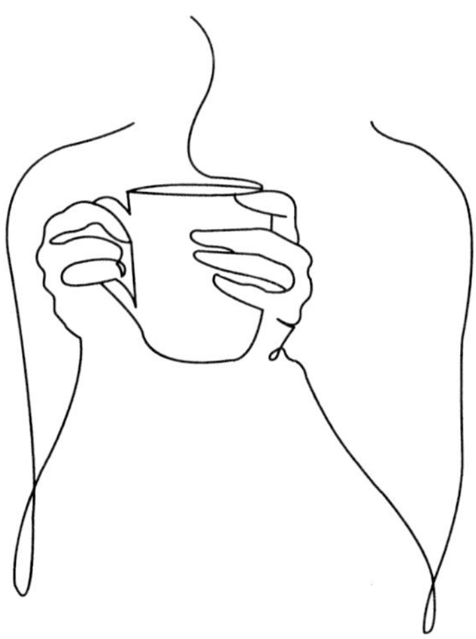

"If you treat people right they will treat you right ninety percent of the time."

"There are many ways of going forward,
but only one way of standing still."

PRESIDENTS ARE SELECTED, NOT ELECTED

"It is common sense to take a method and try it.
If it fails, admit it frankly and try another.
But above all, try something."

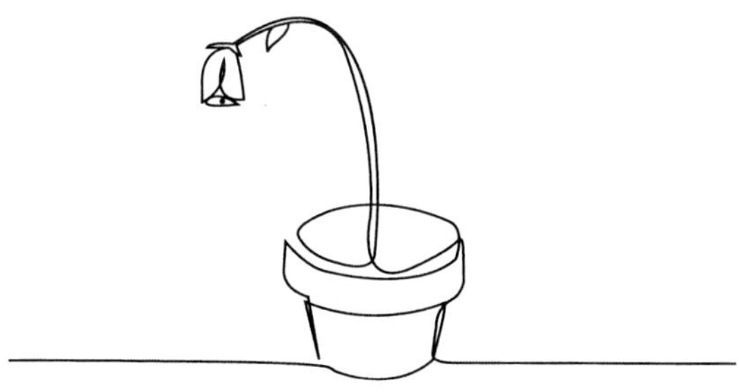

*"Men are not prisoners of fate,
but only prisoners of their own minds."*

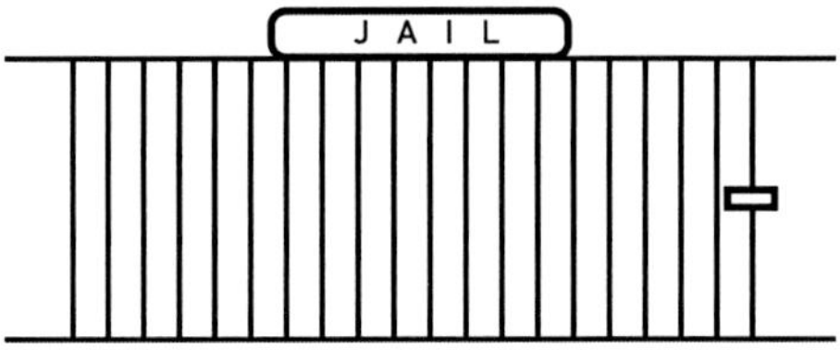

BE
SINCERE,
BE
BRIEF,
BE
SEATED

"A conservative is a man with two perfectly good legs who, however, has never learned to walk forward."

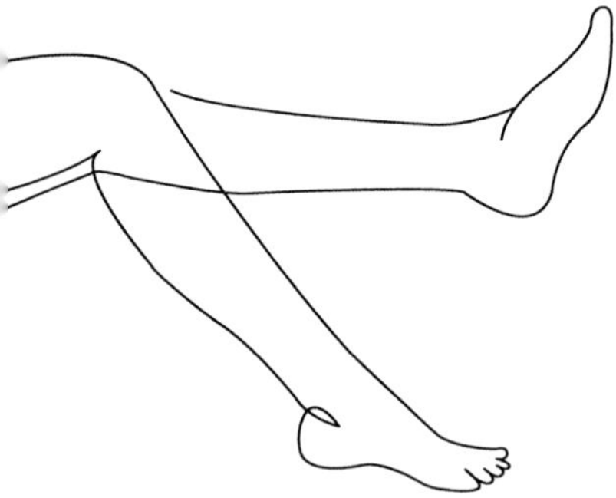

"We have always known that heedless self interest was bad morals, we now know that it is bad economics."

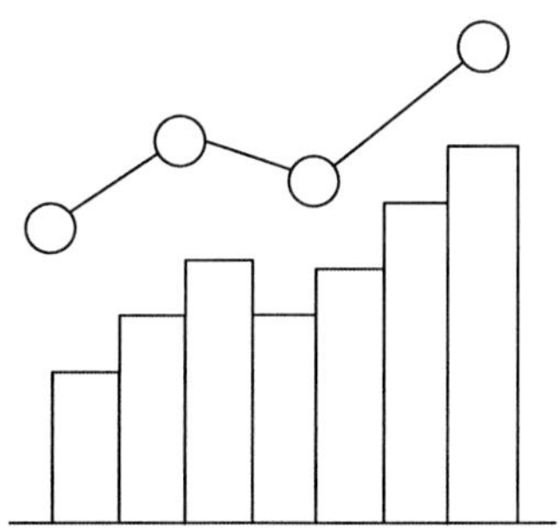

"Freedom means the supremacy of human rights everywhere. Our support goes to those who struggle to gain those rights and keep them. Our strength is our unity of purpose. To that high concept there can be no end save victory."

REPETITION
DOES
NOT
TRANSFORM
A
LIE
INTO
A
TRUTH

"The first truth is that the liberty of a democracy is not safe if the people tolerate the growth of private power to a point where it becomes stronger than their democratic state itself. That, in its essence, is fascism ownership of government by an individual, by a group, or by any other controlling private power Among us today a concentration of private power without equal in history is growing."

"It isn't sufficient just to want - you've got to ask yourself what you are going to do to get the things you want."

"In these days of difficulty,
we Americans everywhere must and
shall choose the path of social justice...,
the path of faith, the path of hope,
and the path of love toward our fellow man."

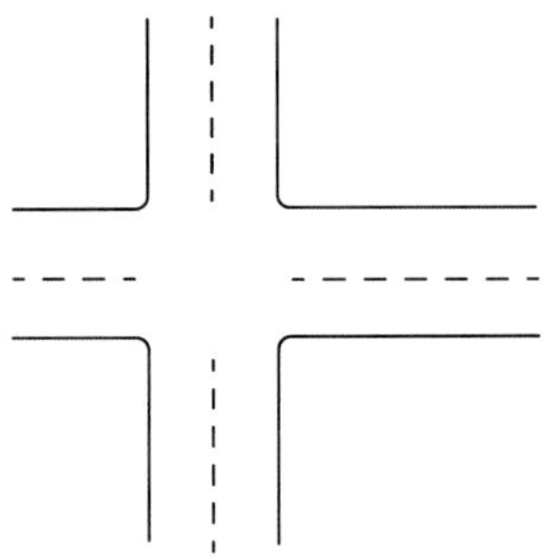

"Human kindness has never weakened the stamina or softened the fiber of a free people. A nation does not have to be cruel to be tough."

"The Truth is found when men (and Women) are free to pursue it."

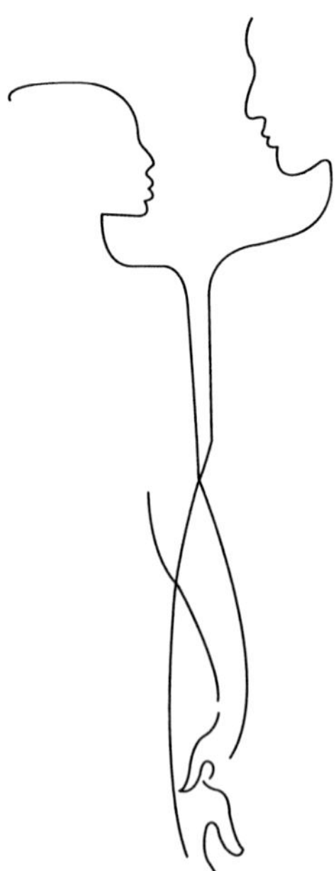

"A war of ideas can no more be won without books than a naval war can be won without ships. Books, like ships, have the toughest armor, the longest cruising range, and mount the most powerful guns."

"Better the occasional faults of a government that lives in a spirit of charity than the consistent omissions of a government frozen in the ice of its own indifference."

WAR
IS
YOUNG
MEN
DYING
AND
OLD
MEN
TALKING

"Competition has been shown to be useful
up to a certain point and no further,
but cooperation, which is the thingwe must strive for today,
begins where competition leaves off."

“True individual freedom cannot exist without economic security and independence. People who are hungry and out of a job are the stuff of which dictatorships are made.Freedom”

"I have seen war. I have seen war on land and sea.
I have seen blood running from the wounded.
I have seen men coughing out their gassed lungs.
I have seen the dead in the mud.
I have seen cities destroyed.
I have seen 200 limping, exhausted men come
out of line—the survivors of a regiment of 1,000
that went forward 48 hours before.
I have seen children starving.
I have seen the agony of mothers and wives.
I hate war."

"Great power involves great responsibility"

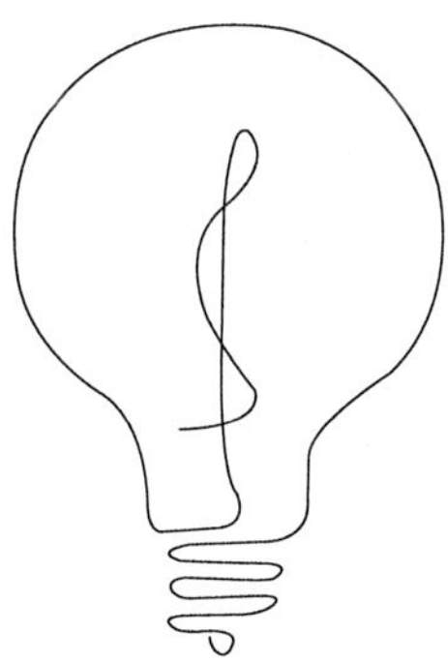

"I think we consider too much the luck of the early bird and not enough the bad luck of the early worm."

"We cannot always build a future for our youth, but we can always build our youth for the future."

"You are only an extra in everyone else's play."

"Those who have long enjoyed such privileges as we enjoy forget in time that men have died to win them."

"In the truest sense,
freedom cannot be bestowed;
it must be achieved."

"A Radical is a man with both feet firmly planted in the air.
A Conservative is a man with two perfectly good legs who,
however, has never learned to walk forward.
A Reactionary is a somnambulist walking backwards.
A Liberal is a man who uses his legs and his hands at
the behest at the command of his head."

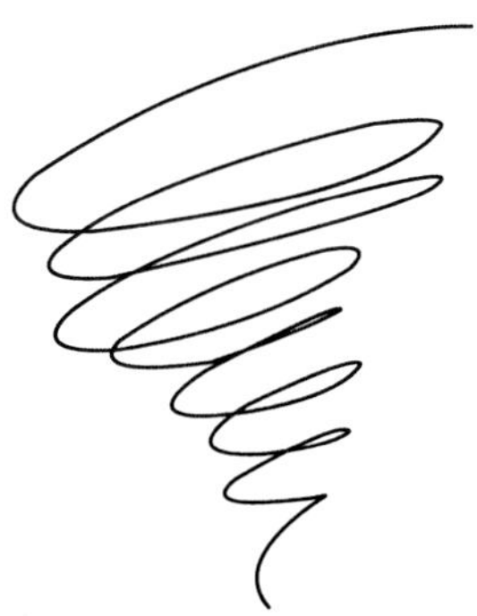

"The real truth of the matter is,
as you and I know,
that a financial element in the large centers has owned the government of the U.S. since the days of Andrew Jackson."

"There is nothing so American as our national parks.
The scenery and the wildlife are native.
The fundamental idea behind the parks is native.
It is, in brief, that the country belongs to the people,
that it is in process of making for the enrichment of
the lives of all of us. The parks stand as
the outward symbal of the great human principle."

"For nearly four years you have had an Administration
which instead of twirling its thumbs has rolled up its sleeves.
We will keep our sleeves rolled up.
We had to struggle with the old enemies of peace business
and financial monopoly, speculation, reckless banking, class
antagonism, sectionalism, war profiteering.
They had begun to consider the Government of the
United States as a mere appendage to their own affairs.
We know now that Government by organized money is
just as dangerous as Government by organized mob."

"Organized money hates me and I welcome their hatred!"

"Taxes, after all,
are dues that we pay for the privileges of
membership in an organized society."

"In politics, nothing happens by accident.
If it happens, you can bet it was planned that way."

"The only sure bulwark of continuing liberty is a government strong enough to protect the interests of the people, and a people strong enough and well enough informed to maintain its sovereign control over the government."

"First of all, let me assert my firm belief that the only thing we have to fear is fear itself nameless, unreasoning, unjustified terror which paralyzes needed efforts to convert retreat into advance."

"There should be no bitterness or hate where the sole thought is the welfare of the United States of America. No man can occupy the office of President without realizing that he is President of all the people."

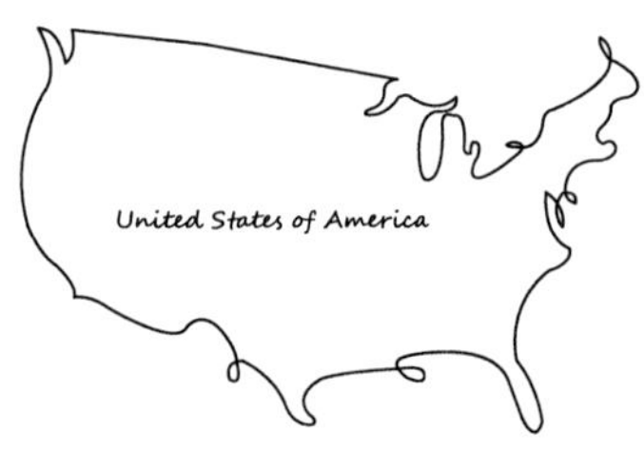

"We and all others who believe in freedom as deeply as we do, would rather die on our feet than live on our knees."

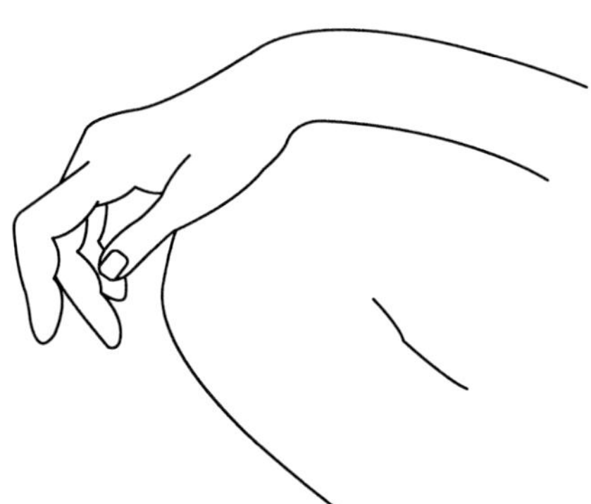

"Today we are faced with the pre-eminent fact that if civilization is to survive, we must cultivate the science of human relationships, the ability of all peoples of all kins to live together and to work together in the same world at peace."

"It is the purpose of government to see that not only the legitimate interests of the few are protected but that the welfare and rights of the many are conserved."

"I sometimes think that the saving grace of America lies in the fact that the overwhelming majority of Americans are possessed of two great qualities a sense of humor and a sense of proportion."

I
LOVE
IT
I
JUST
LOVE
IT

"The country needs and unless I mistake its temper
the country demands bold persistent experimentation.
It is common sense to take a method and try it
If it fails admit it frankly and try another.
But above all try something."

"More striking still, it appeared that,
if the process of concentration goes on at the same rate,
at the end of another century we shall have all American
industry controlled by a dozen corporations and run
by perhaps a hundred men. Put plainly,
we are steering a steady course toward economic oligarchy,
if we are not there already."

*"We have learned that we cannot live alone,
at peace; that our own well-being is dependent on
the well-being of nations far away.
We have learned that we must live as men,
and not as ostriches nor as dogs in the manger.
We have learned to be citizens of the world,
members of the human community."*

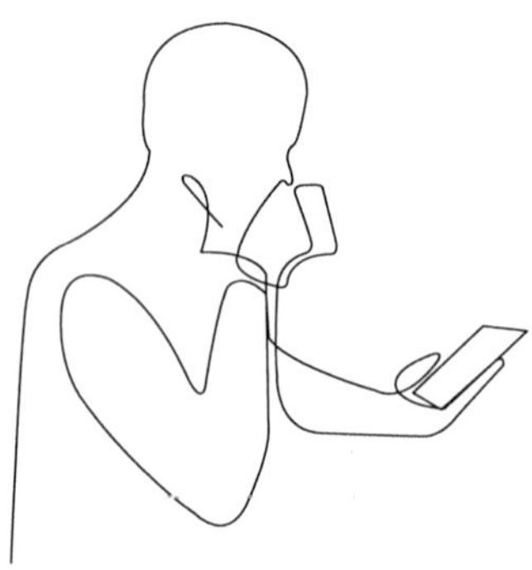

"Never underestimate a man who overestimates himself."

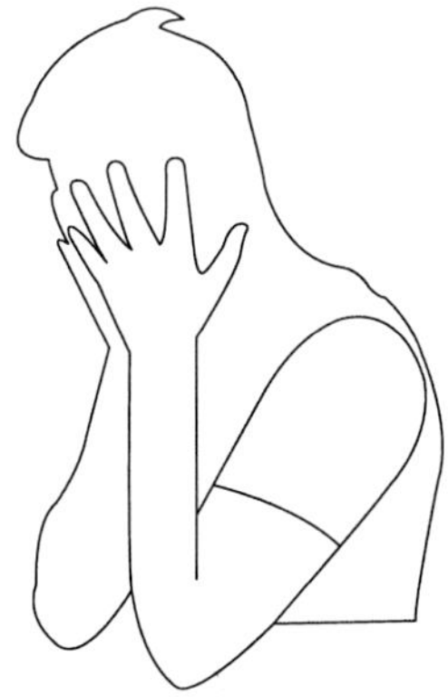

"Physical strength can never permanently withstand the impact of spiritual force."

"The essence of our struggle is that men shall be free."

"Some people can never understand that you have to wait, even for the best of things, until the right time comes."

"Do something. If it works, do more of it.
If it doesn't, do something else."

"If the fires of freedom and civil liberties burn low in other lands they must be made brighter in our own. If in other lands the press and books and literature of all kinds are censored we must redouble our efforts here to keep them free. If in other lands the eternal truths of the past are threatened by intolerance we must provide a safe place for their perpetuation."

"There is a mysterious cycle in human events. To some generations much is given. Of other generations much is expected. This generation of Americans has a rendezvous with destiny. In this world of ours in other lands, there are some people, who, in times past, have lived and fought for freedom, and seem to have grown too weary to carry on the fight. They have sold their heritage of freedom for the illusion of a living. They have yielded their democracy.

I believe in my heart that only our success can stir their ancient hope. They begin to know that here in America we are waging a war against want and destitution and economic demoralization. It is more than that; it is a war for the survival of democracy. We are fighting to save a great and precious form of government for ourselves and for the world."

"We must especially beware of that small group of selfish men who would clip the wings of the American Eagle in order to feather their own nests."

*"We have faith that future generations will know that here,
in the middle of the twentieth century,
there came a time when men of good will found a way
to unite, and produce, and fight to destroy the forces of
ignorance, and intolerance, and slavery, and war."*

"I venture the challenging statement that if American democracy ceases to move forward as a living force, seeking day and night by peaceful means to better the lot of our citizens, fascism will grow in strength in our land."

"Confidence thrives on honesty, on honor,
on the sacredness of obligations,
on faithful protection and on unselfish performance.
Without them it cannot live."

"We had to struggle with the old enemies of peace business and financial monopoly, speculation, reckless banking, class antagonism, sectionalism, war profiteering.
They had begun to consider the government of the United States as a mere appendage to their own affairs and we know now that a government by organized money is just as bad as a government by organized mob."

"We have always held to the hope, the belief, the conviction that there is a better life, a better world, beyond the horizon."

"It's a terrible thing to look over your shoulder when you are trying to lead and to find no one there."

"As a nation we may take pride in the fact that we are softhearted; but we cannot afford to be soft-headed"

PRIDE

"We know that equality of individual ability has never existed and never will, but we do insist that equality of opportunity still must be sought."

"There is a mysterious cycle in human events.
To some generations much is given.
Of other generations much is expected."

"Cooperation, which is the thing we must strive for today, begins where competition leaves off."

"It seems to me to be equally plain that no business which depends for existence on paying less than livin wages to its workers has any right to continue in this country. By "business" I mean the whole of commerce as well as the whole of industry; by workers I mean all workers, the white collar class as well as the men in overalls; and by living wages I mean more than a bare subsistence level-I mean the wages of decent living."

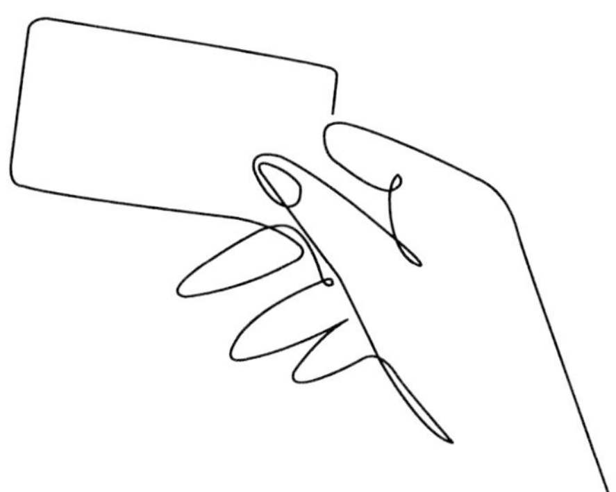

"We all know that books burn, yet we have the greater knowledge that books cannot be killed by fire. People die, but books never die. No man and no force can put thought in a concentration camp forever. No man and no force can take from the world the books that embody man's eternal fight against tyranny of every kind."

"It is not the critic who counts; not the man who points out how the strong man stumbles, or where the doer of deeds could have done them better. The credit belongs to the man who is actually in the arena, whose face is marred by dust and sweat and blood; who strives valiantly; who errs, who comes short again and again, because there is no effort without error and shortcoming; but who does actually strive to do the deeds; who knows great enthusiasms, the great devotions; who spends himself in a worthy cause; who at the best knows in the end the triumph of high achievement, and who at the worst, if he fails, at least fails while daring greatly, so that his place shall never be with those cold and timid souls who neither know victory nor defeat."

"The nation that destroys its soil destroys itself."

"We have nothing to fear but fear itself"

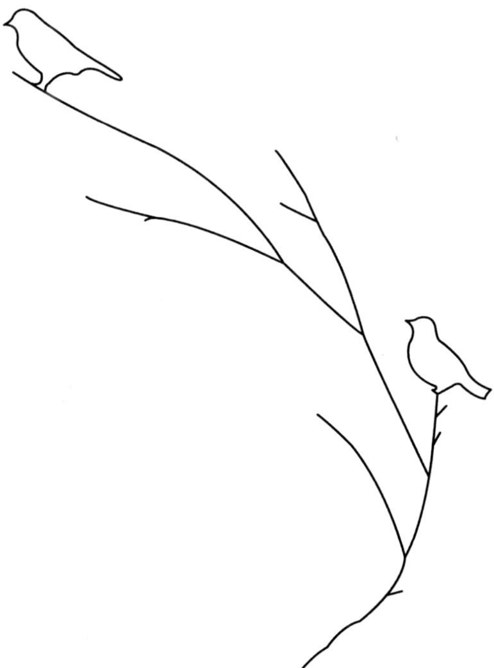

"The lessons of history, confirmed by the evidence immediately before me, show conclusively that continued dependence upon relief induces a spiritual and moral disintegration fundamentally destructive to the national fiber. To dole out relief in this way is to administer a narcotic, a subtle destroyer of the human spirit. It is inimical to the dictates of sound policy. It is in violation of the traditions of America."

"It is an unfortunate human failing that a full pocketbook often groans more loudly than an empty stomach."

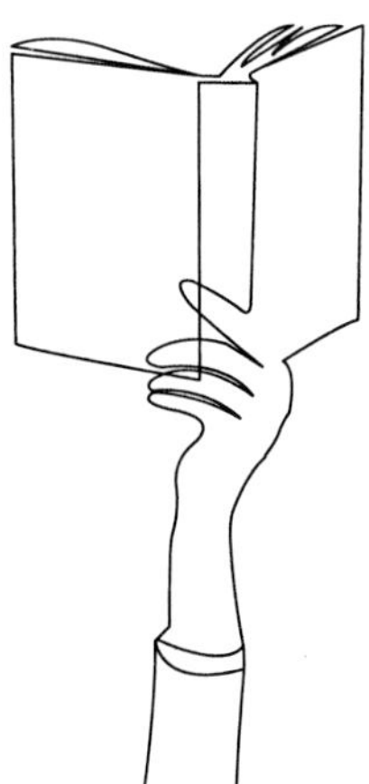

"It is to the real advantage of every producer, every manufacturer and every merchant to cooperate in the improvement of working conditions, because the best customer of American industry is the well-paid worker."

"Nobody will ever deprive the American people of the right to vote except the American people themselves and the only way they could do this is by not voting."

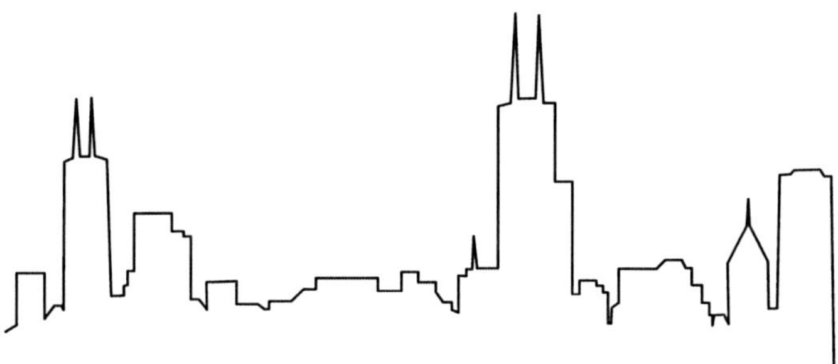

"If we will not prepare to give all that
we have and that all that we are to preserve
Christian civilization in our land,
we shall go to destruction."

"I see one-third of a nation ill housed, ill clad, ill nourished...the test of our progress is not whether we add more to the abundance of those who have much; it is whether we provide enough for those that have too little"

"The history of the last half century is accordingly in large measure a history of financial titans, whose methods were not scrutinized with too much care and who were honored in proportion as they produced the results, irrespective of the means they used."

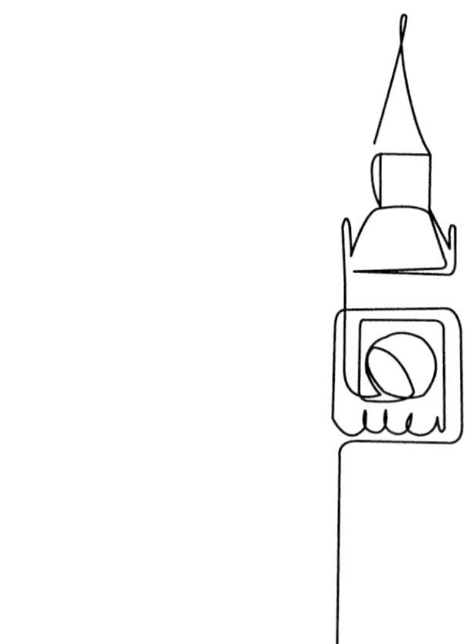

"The alternate domination of one faction over another, sharpened by the spirit of revenge, natural to party dissension, which in different ages and countries has perpetrated the most horrid enormities, is itself a frightful despotism."

"Remember, remember always, that all of us,
and you and I especially,
are descended from immigrants and revolutionaries."

"Good government should maintain the balance where every individual may have a place if he will take it, where every individual may find safety if he wishes it, where every individual may attain such power as his ability permits, consistent with his assuming the accompanying responsibility."

"People, like charity, begins at home."

"One cannot always build the future for our youth, but we can build our youth for the future."

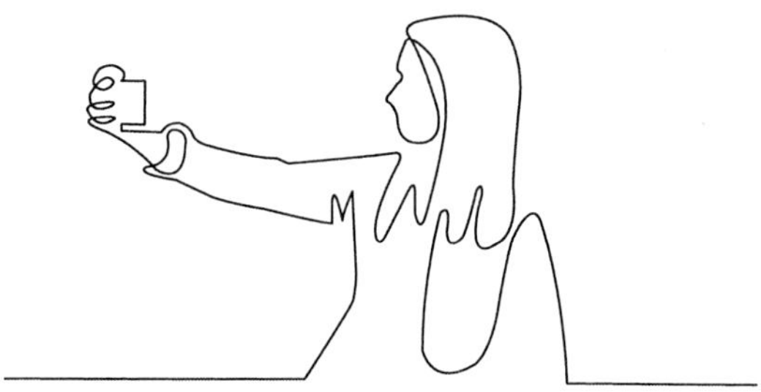

"True regulation is for the equal benefit of the consumer and the investor, and the only man who will suffer from true regulation is the speculator or the unscrupulous promoter who levies tribute equally from the man who buys the service and from the man who invests his savings in this great industry."

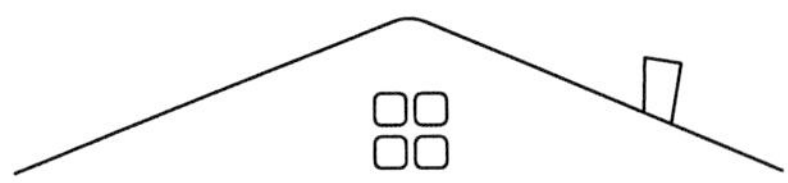

"Hitler built a fortress around Europe, but he forgot to put a roof on it."

"The only thing we have to fear is fear itself nameless, unreasoning, unjustified terror which paralyzes needed efforts to convert retreat into advance."